Rookie
Read-About® Geography

Latitude and Longitude

By Rebecca Aberg

Consultant
Jeanne Clidas, Ph.D.
National Reading Consultant
and
Professor of Reading, SUNY Brockport

SCHOLASTIC INC.

New York   Toronto   London   Auckland   Sydney
Mexico City   New Delhi   Hong Kong   Buenos Aires

Designer: Herman Adler Design
Photo Researcher: Caroline Anderson
The artwork on the cover shows the latitude and longitude lines on the globe.

ISBN 0-516-25541-X

12 11 10 9 8 7 6 5 4   5 6 7 8 9/0
Printed in the U.S.A.   61

First Scholastic printing, October 2004

What are the lines for
on a map or globe?

3

The lines on a map or globe help you read the map or globe.

These lines make a grid. Some of the lines go across. Some of the lines go up and down.

Look at this map. It also uses a grid.

Do you see Bear Cave?

To find it, follow line 2 down. Follow line C across. Bear Cave is where lines 2 and C meet.

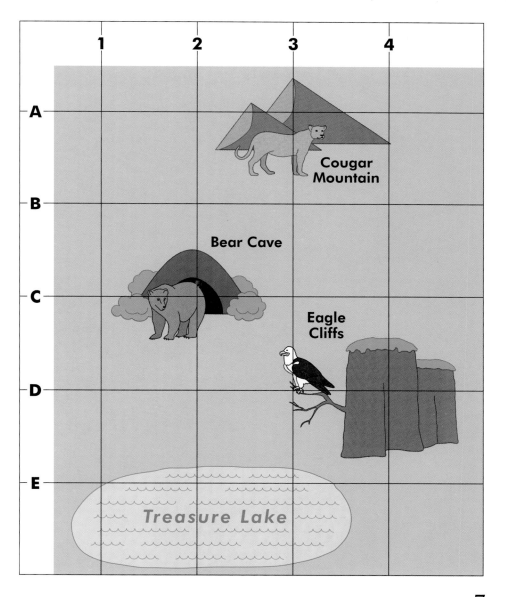

Cougar Mountain

Bear Cave

Eagle Cliffs

Treasure Lake

7

8

A long time ago, map-makers decided to use a grid. They drew lines on maps and globes of the world.

The lines helped explorers and others to find their way. Explorers are people who travel to new places.

We still use the same lines today. We call them latitude (LAT-uh-tood) and longitude (LON-juh-tood) lines.

The lines are numbered and have a degree sign (°) after them.

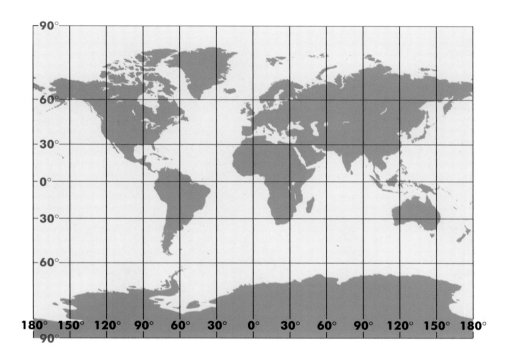

11

12

Latitude lines go across
a map or around a globe.
They run east and west.

Latitude lines are shortest at the North and South Poles. They get longer as they reach the middle of the earth.

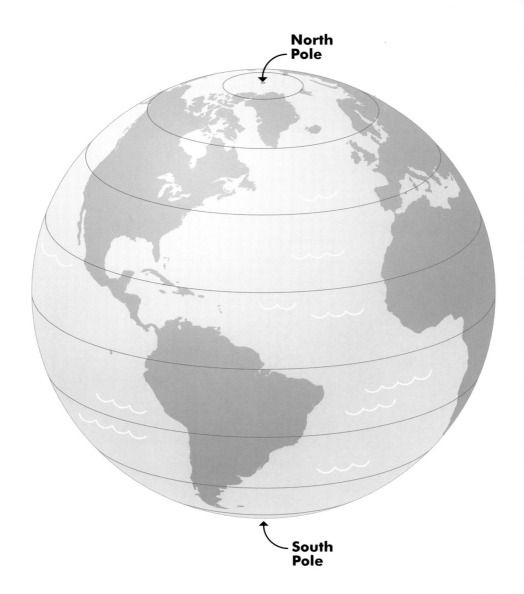

North Pole

South Pole

15

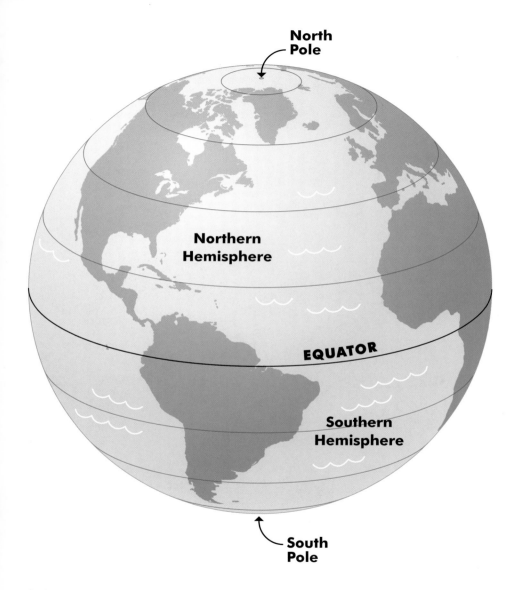

North Pole

Northern Hemisphere

EQUATOR

Southern Hemisphere

South Pole

16

The equator (i-KWAY-tur) is the latitude line that circles the middle of the earth. It divides Earth into northern and southern hemispheres (HEM-uhss-fihrz).

A hemisphere is half
a sphere.

An orange cut in half
has two hemispheres.

19

Longitude lines go up and down on a map or globe. They run north and south.

Longitude lines get closer together at the top or bottom of a map or globe. They meet at the North and South Poles.

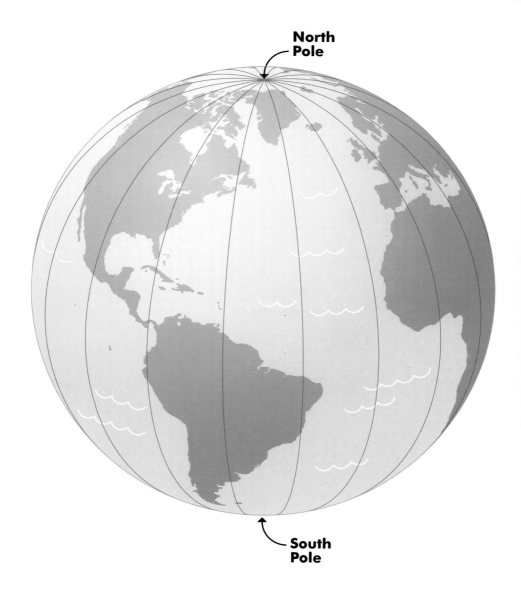

North Pole

South Pole

23

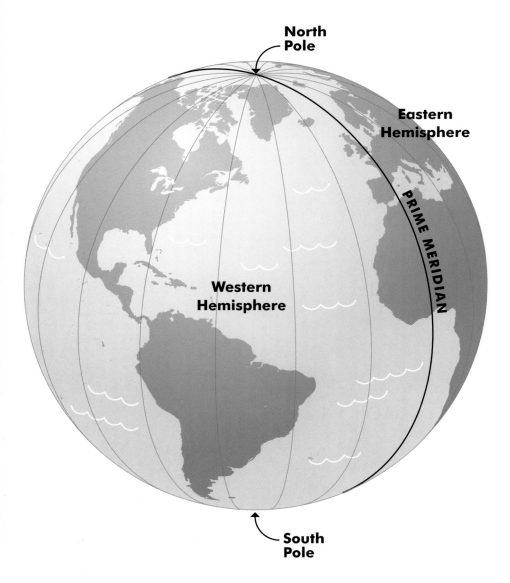

24

The Prime Meridian
(muh-RID-ee-uhn) is
the first longitude line.
All other longitude lines
are numbered starting there.

The Prime Meridian
divides Earth into
eastern and western
hemispheres.

Latitude and longitude lines are important to sailors and pilots. They use the lines to find their way. You can use these lines, too.

Look at this picture. The fingers are pointing to a place. What is the name of the place? What is the latitude?

Use a map to find out!

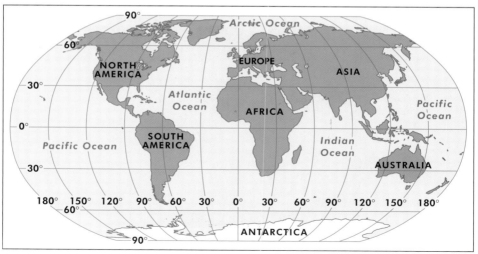

Words You Know

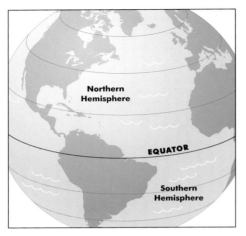

Equator

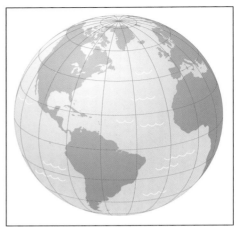

grid

hemisphere

30

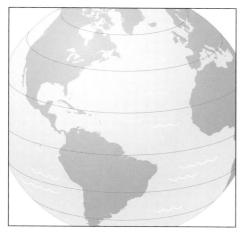

latitude

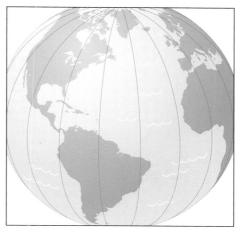

longitude

pilots

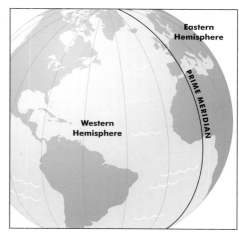

Eastern
Hemisphere

PRIME MERIDIAN

Western
Hemisphere

Prime Meridian

Index

About the Author

Rebecca Aberg lives in Wisconsin and teaches elementary school. She has written more than 20 books. Rebecca enjoys learning as much as she enjoys teaching others.

Photo Credits

Photographs © 2003: Corbis Images: 8; Leslie Barbour: 3, 12, 20, 29; The Image Works/Norbert Schiller: 26; Visuals Unlimited/David Wrobel: 19.

Illustrations by XNR Productions